**Please check all items for damages
before leaving the Library.
Thereafter you will be held
responsible for all injuries
to items beyond reasonable wear.**

SUPER CUTE!

Baby
Tigers

by Christina Leaf

BELLWETHER MEDIA • MINNEAPOLIS, MN

Note to Librarians, Teachers, and Parents:

Blastoff! Readers are carefully developed by literacy experts and combine standards-based content with developmentally appropriate text.

Level 1 provides the most support through repetition of high-frequency words, light text, predictable sentence patterns, and strong visual support.

Level 2 offers early readers a bit more challenge through varied simple sentences, increased text load, and less repetition of high-frequency words.

Level 3 advances early-fluent readers toward fluency through increased text and concept load, less reliance on visuals, longer sentences, and more literary language.

Level 4 builds reading stamina by providing more text per page, increased use of punctuation, greater variation in sentence patterns, and increasingly challenging vocabulary.

Level 5 encourages children to move from "learning to read" to "reading to learn" by providing even more text, varied writing styles, and less familiar topics.

Whichever book is right for your reader, Blastoff! Readers are the perfect books to build confidence and encourage a love of reading that will last a lifetime!

This edition first published in 2015 by Bellwether Media, Inc.

No part of this publication may be reproduced in whole or in part without written permission of the publisher. For information regarding permission, write to Bellwether Media, Inc., Attention: Permissions Department, 5357 Penn Avenue South, Minneapolis, MN 55419.

Library of Congress Cataloging-in-Publication Data

Leaf, Christina, author.
  Baby Tigers / by Christina Leaf.
    pages cm. – (Blastoff! Readers. Super Cute!)
  Summary: "Developed by literacy experts for students in kindergarten through grade three, this book introduces baby tigers to young readers through leveled text and related photos."– Provided by publisher.
  Audience: Ages 5-8.
  Audience: K to grade 3.
  Includes bibliographical references and index.
  ISBN 978-1-62617-173-2 (hardcover : alk. paper)
  1. Tiger–Infancy–Juvenile literature. I. Title. II. Series: Blastoff! Readers. 1, Super Cute!
  QL737.C23L424 2015
  599.75613'92–dc23
                          2014034760

Table of Contents

Tiger Cubs!

Baby tigers are called cubs. They are born in **dens**.

A female has a **litter** of two to six cubs. They stay in the den for two months.

Life With Mom

Newborn cubs need mom for everything. She carries them with her teeth.

She also **nurses** them. Older cubs eat **solid food**.

A Lot to Learn

Tiger cubs have a lot to learn. Mom teaches them how to hunt.

Cubs chase
one another
to practice.

Then they **wrestle**. They **growl** as they play-fight.

Sometimes the cubs practice an **ambush**. They **pounce** on mom.

Young cubs also learn how to swim. They love water. Jump in!

Glossary

ambush—a surprise attack

dens—places where tiger cubs are born and raised

growl—to make a low, angry sound

litter—a group of babies that are born together

newborn—just recently born

nurses—feeds a baby her milk

pounce—to jump on suddenly

solid food—food other than milk; solid food for tigers is meat such as deer and wild pig.

wrestle—to fight in a playful way

To Learn More

AT THE LIBRARY

Jenkins, Martin. *Can We Save the Tiger?*
Somerville, Mass.: Candlewick Press, 2011.

Leaf, Christina. *Baby Lions*. Minneapolis,
Minn.: Bellwether Media, 2014.

Zobel, Derek. *Tigers*. Minneapolis, Minn.:
Bellwether Media, 2012.

ON THE WEB

Learning more about tigers
is as easy as 1, 2, 3.

1. Go to www.factsurfer.com.

2. Enter "tigers" into the search box.

3. Click the "Surf" button and you will see a
   list of related web sites.

With factsurfer.com, finding more information
is just a click away.

Index

The images in this book are reproduced through the courtesy of: Martin Harvey/ Corbis, front cover; Michael Krabs/ Glow Images, pp. 4-5; Gerard Lacz Images/ SuperStock, pp. 6-7, 10-11; Eric Gevaert, pp. 8-9; Suzi Eszterhas/ Corbis, pp. 12-13; Chris Godfrey Wildlife Photography/ Alamy, pp. 14-15; Jens Meyer/ AP Images/ Corbis, pp. 16-17, 20-21; M. Robbemont, pp. 18-19.